HOLY WIT

BY THE SAME AUTHOR

There is a time to . . .   James Clarke Publishers 1971
Marriage Questions Today   St. Andrew Press 1975
Doubts are not enough   St. Andrew Press 1982

HOLY WIT

Selected and Compiled by

Rev. James A. Simpson

Illustrated by TURNBULL

GORDON WRIGHT PUBLISHING
25 MAYFIELD ROAD, EDINBURGH EH9 2NQ
SCOTLAND

Reprinted 1986.

British Library Cataloguing in Publication Data

Simpson, James A.
  Holy Wit.
  1. Christian life — Anecdotes, facetiae,
  satire, etc.
  I. Title
  248.4   BV4517

  ISBN 0-903065-55-X

Typeset by Gordon Wright Publishing Ltd.
Printed by Billing & Sons Ltd. Worcester.

Contents

To Sally Macaskill
with Love

'It is the test of good religion whether you can make a joke of it.'
G.K. Chesterton.

'The sound of laughter has always semed to me the most civilised music in the universe.'
Peter Ustinov.

Introduction

Ministers are often libelled on television by being depicted as morose, humourless creatures who cast a disparaging gaze on the lighter and pleasanter aspects of life. The Vicar in *To the Manor Born*, and the padre in *Colditz* were so wet you could have wrung them out! For them, as for that other B.B.C. prophet of doom, the Rev. I.M. Jolly (as portrayed by Rikki Fulton), religion is anything but a laughing matter.

In the parishes of Britain there are a few priests, ministers and rabbis who look and speak like undertakers, but fortunately they are in the minority. The majority have an eye for the recurring comedy of things. They regularly exercise their 'chuckle' muscles. Today most of the leading figures in the church and many lesser known ones, are masters of the witty remark and superlative story tellers of humorous anecdotes, often against themselves.

Over the years I have amused myself by collecting anecdotes associated with the clergy in Britain and America. Sometimes witty remarks or humorous happenings, originally associated with an ordinary parish minister, have later been fictitiously linked with some prominent churchman in order to heighten the humour. This being so, it is not always possible to guarantee the authenticity of such stories, but I have genuinely tried in this volume to limit myself to those which I know to be true, and those which at least appear to have the ring of truth about them. My warm thanks are due to many churchmen of different denominations, including archbishops, bishops and moderators, who graciously responded to my invitation to share with a wider audience, humorous incidents from their own experience.

I hope there is many a good laugh in this book, and no irreverence.

James A. Simpson
Cathedral Manse
Dornoch.

Clerical Errors

A Dorset minister was surprised to receive a typed note listing possible hymns for a funeral, beginning with *Amazing Grave* (Grace).

An American tells how on St. Andrew's Day, when a Scottish preacher was in their pulpit, an inspired misprint appeared in the Order of Service.
Prelude: *Come Saviour of the Heather* (Heathen).

The Very Rev. Dr. Archie Craig tells how in notes which he had prepared for an address to a Woman's Temperance Association, he discovered he had typed, 'And now two final pints.'
The same instrument which typed notes for an address at a girl's school prize-giving, referred to the headmistress as 'an old fiend' (friend).

A Glasgow church newsletter announced, 'There will be a "Parish Sin-a-long" (Sing-a-long) on Sunday at 7.30pm.'
In another magazine an appeal for additional choristers was headed, 'Sinners wanted for the choir.'

An English Church magazine announced that Mr. Kennedy had taken over the ruining (running) of the Scouts from Mr. Black.

Writing thanking all the secretaries of the various church organisations for their careful preparations for the winter's work, the minister expressed the hope that all their plans would duly come to friction (fruition).

The birth notice in the local newspaper read, 'To Mr. and Mrs. John Mackay, a son, a bother (brother) for Susan.'

In a wedding report it was stated that 'the three tiered wedding cage (cake) had been made by the bride.'

Another report stated that the town's festival week service would be conducted by the priest, the minister and the rabbit (rabbi).

A nine-year-old returned from convent school the Monday before Easter and announced that this was to be the last week of the school year. Her mother told her she must have made a mistake. 'But Mummy, it's true. Here's a note from the teacher.' When her mother read it, she discovered the typist had accidentally inserted a comma. 'The school will be closed for Good, Friday.'

A note on the notice-board at a Synod meeting caused considerable hilarity. 'There will be an infirmal (informal) meeting tomorrow of those ordained prior to 1939.'

From a church bulletin in a small South Carolina town: 'There will be a meeting of Deacons next Sunday morning. It will be gin with breakfast at 7.30 a.m.'

Holy Horrors

In moments of extreme confusion ministers have spoken of:
'the evening service being halled in the hell below' (held in the hall below).
'my text being from the Juke of Bob' (Book of Job)
'Jordan baptising Jesus in the John' (John baptising Jesus in the Jordan).
'the poets Kelly and Sheets' (Shelley and Keats).
'Jesus as the shoving leopard' (loving Shepherd).

The renowned Dr. Spooner, himself an Anglican clergyman, spoke of:
'the tearful chidings of the gospel' (cheerful tidings).
'a person who had received a blushing crow' (crushing blow).
'how though people differ in rank and station, at death they are all brought to a red devil' (dead level).

A commissioner to the General Assembly received a letter addressed:

Rev. Hugh Macdonald,
The General Ass of the Church of Scotland,
The Mound, Edinburgh.

A Sutherland minister who was appealing for funds for the training of the ministry said, 'I hope you will all give generously for our students are very poorly circumcised.'
The same minister said at a wedding service, 'We are gathered here today to witness the consummation (consecration) of this marriage.'

One minister intimated the hymn, *From Iceland's Greasy Mountains* (Greenland's Icy Mountains), while another announced there would be a presentation to Mary Forbes who was going as a bookmaker (book-keeper) to the mission field.

Numerous have been the verbal slips on the occasion of ministers moving or retiring.

'Mr. Clarke has been the incumbrance (incumbent) here for forty years.'
Another parishioner explained to a friend that their minister was leaving and the office-bearers had decided to give him a wee bit of momentum (memento).

When asked why her parents had changed from the Presbyterian to the Episcopal Church, one teenager replied, 'My mother likes the Episcopal lethargy (liturgy) better.'

F.F. Bruce of Sheffield University in his book *The Spreading Flame* tells the story of the early history of the Church. Once at a dinner he was introduced as the man who had written *The Flaming Spread.*

An Edinburgh minister was horrified when he was quoted in the local newspaper as having expressed his delight with the 'nudist play in the church hall'. What he had actually said was 'I am delighted with the new display in the church hall.'

The Rev. Mr. Cassells tells of addressing a church meeting. Afterwards a lady who had been present was ecstatic in her appreciation 'Oh Mr. Cassells, that was wonderful. Every word you said was superfluous.'

A minister was conducting his first prison service. Unfortunately he did not give sufficient thought as to how he should begin. Come the time for the service to start, he said, 'I'm so glad you are all here today.'

An English conference centre, much used by church groups, has as its motto: 'There are no problems, only opportunities.'
One day, a minister who had not long booked in, presented himself again at the reception. When he said he had a problem, the receptionist responded with a smile. 'Sir, we do not have problems here, only opportunities.' 'Call it what you like', said the vicar, 'but there is a woman in my room.'

An Irish newspaper reported how one Sunday in an Irish village, three Protestant women visited a packed Roman Catholic Church. Recognising them and wishing to show respect, the priest whispered to his server, 'Three chairs for the Protestant ladies.' The server jumped to his feet and shouted, 'Three *cheers* for the Protestant ladies.' The congregation rose and responded heartily.

A Dr. Smith was upset when in a newspaper advertisement the title of his sermon appeared as 'Why I believe in immorality', instead of immortality.

Misquotations

If pollution is uncontrolled, 'the muck shall inherit the earth.'

Speaking of weapons of war one minister said, 'May they rust in peace.'

'Faith, hope and clarity, but the greatest of these is clarity' (charity).

The sixth commandment is 'Humour your father and mother.'

'And they brought unto Jesus a penny. And he saith unto them, "Whose is this subscription?" ' (superscription).

Samson was the original press agent. He took two columns and brought the house down.

Eve was the first person to eat herself out of house and home.

Several sports are mentioned in the Bible:
Cricket: We are told Peter stood up before the eleven and was bold (bowled).
Tennis: We are told that David served in the courts of Saul.
Motor-bike racing: We are told that David's Triumph was heard throughout all Israel.

A minister who had taken a week's holiday to look after his two young children while his wife was in hospital, discovered just how much time mothers spend tidying up after their children, putting away their clothes and toys. He later confided that Paul's words, 'When I became a man I put away childish things. . . . ' had taken on a new meaning for him.

For centuries the theological thinking of the Roman Church has been closely tied to the writing of Thomas Aquinas. At the time of the Second Vatican Council, one religious commentator who regarded this close tie as inhibiting necessary reforms, suggested that it might be a good idea if the Council were to close with the Pope, Cardinals and Bishops joining hands and singing, 'Should Auld Aquinas be forgot . . .'

The reviewer of a book by one of the 'Death of God' philosophers, chose as the title of his review, 'There is no God and Jesus is His Son'.

It was a bitterly cold day. The country church was anything but warm. The minister having intimated his text, 'Many are called but few are chosen' (Matt 22 v 14) added with a twinkle in his eye, 'Perhaps I should slightly change it to "Many are cauld, but few are frozen".'

A minister who is one of Scotland's finest after-dinner speakers was once humorously referred to as 'the thief of bad gags' (Baghdad).

Commenting on New York City's awesome traffic situation, Billy Graham said, 'The only people here are the quick and the dead.'

When a minister rehearses his sermon, is he practising what he preaches?

In the *Catholic Review* under a picture of a priest's collar there were the words, 'White-collar workers needed.'

An American evangelist once ended his radio broadcast by exhorting his listeners to 'go and cast their bread upon the waters'. Before introducing the next programme the radio announcer said, 'This is the national breadcasting corporation.'

The following note was found taped to a faulty machine at a training college for Baptist ministers. 'This machine filleth with water, but "it toileth not, neither doth it spin".'

A sign in the foyer of a cinema which was showing Cecil B. De Mille's epic film *The Ten Commandments*, read, 'Thou shalt not smoke.'

Sir Leary Constantine, the former West Indian cricketer, was later appointed Ambassador to London. He was invited on one occasion to be the guest speaker at a London dinner. In introducing him the Master of Ceremonies said, 'My Lords, Ladies and Gentlemen, pray for the silence of Sir Leary Constantine', instead of 'pray silence for' ... Rising slowly to his feet, Sir Leary said, 'Ladies and gentlemen, your prayers have been answered.' ... and momentarily sat down.

When a parishioner told Bishop Feaver of Peterborough that there was nothing he liked better than canoeing on Rutland Water, the Bishop replied, 'Canoeing in this weather! I'd rather canoodle any day.'

Down With Your Heads

Humorous Graces

Down with your head
Up with your paws
Thank the good Lord
For the use of your jaws.

Heavenly Father bless us
And keep us all alive
There's ten of us to dinner
And not enough for five.

O Lord, wha blest the loaves and fishes
Look down upon these twa wee dishes
And tho' the tatties be but sma'
Lord mak them plenty for us a'
But if our stomachs they do fill
'Twill be another miracle.

The graduation banquet was about to begin when the master of ceremonies was informed that the invited clergyman would not be able to attend. The M.C. quickly asked the guest speaker if he would say grace. The speaker rose, bowed his head and said, 'There being no clergyman present, let us thank God.'

Mr. J.L.Toole, a well known actor of by-gone days once attended a church dinner at which he was the only layman present. In virtue of this the Bishop asked if he would be willing to say grace. For a moment Toole was non-plussed, as he could not recall a single one, but just when he had become desperate, there came to mind some words from the prayer-book, which to the amusement of his fellow-diners he repeated, 'O Lord open thou our lips and our mouths will show forth thy praise.'

Father J. Hever of St. Joseph's Church, Belmont, Massachusetts, was asked to say grace at a public banquet in the staid old city of Boston. Expecting the usual kind of ministerial grace, spoken in funereal tones, those present were surprised to hear Father Hever pray:

'Almighty God we are especially happy to make this prayer, and we hope you are to hear it, because we are not in church and we are not in trouble. As a rule when we speak to you we are either kneeling against the background of a stained glass window, or buckling on a life preserver. It is either the routine of religion or the rush call for help. But today it is gloriously different. We are out of church and ready to have a good time. We want you to bless our joy as we meet for a few hours of genial festivity. Bless us O Lord in your goodness, this food that it may be well flavoured, this service that it may be smooth. And if it is not asking too much, keep the speeches short.'

Humour and Prayer

The Rev. Lawrence Whitley was praying one day at the bedside of a sick old lady who had a poodle and a hen-pecked husband. Half-way through the prayer the dog became very agitated and jumped on the bed. 'Get him out George. Get him out', hissed the old lady. The obedient husband, not realising it was the dog she was referring to, took Mr. Whitley firmly by the elbow and made to lead him out of the room!

A Highland minister, not renowned for overworking, prayed one Sunday, at the start of the week of prayer for Christian Unity, for the day when 'there would be one shepherd and one sheep'.

A minister conducting worship at Crathie Kirk in the time of Queen Victoria, transported by the glory of preaching in the Church the Queen had built, prayed fervently: 'Grant that as she grows to be an old woman she may be a new man, and that in all righteous causes she may go forth before her people like a he-goat on the mountains.'

'Father bless us according to our thanklessness, lest thou bless us according to our thankfulness, and we starve.'

18

It was a young people's service. Unknown to me two ladies on their way to church that morning had been bemoaning the fact that they were getting older and putting on weight. My opening prayer, intended for the young people, was not well received by these two ladies. 'We thank you for growing older and bigger every day.'

During a royal occasion in Glasgow Cathedral, the minister, Dr. Lauchlan Maclean Watt, meant to say in his opening prayer, 'Eternal and ever blessed God, in whose hands are the hearts of kings.', but instead prayed, 'Eternal and ever blessed God, in whose hand is the king of hearts.' His bridge friends had difficulty in suppressing their merriment.

At the turn of the century the Rev. David Waters of Moray prayed one Sunday, 'O Lord we pray for the Prince of Wales (Edward V11), and if all we hear of him be true, he much needs our prayers.'

19

A little boy gave a loud shrill whistle during the minister's prayer one Sunday. His mother immediately scolded him saying, 'Why did you do that?' Surprised at getting a row, he said, 'Mummy I asked God to teach me to whistle, and he did just then.'

The late David Watson of York told how after one of his talks, someone came up to him and said, 'David, the best talk I ever heard . . . ' At this point David said, 'I began to pray desperately for enough humility to cope with the effusive praise that was obviously coming.' But the man's sentence ended ' . . . was given by Canon Collins.' David Watson later commented wryly, 'My prayer was answered too quickly for my liking.'

'Grant O God that we may always be right, for thou knowest we will never change our minds.'

'If there is a spark of grace in any heart here, water it, water it.'

'Lord help us to stand for something, lest we fall for anything.' (Peter Marshall).

A member of the Church of Scotland who had read the prayer, 'O Lord grant that we may not be like porridge - stiff, stodgy and hard to stir; but like cornflakes - crisp, fresh and ready to serve' suggested a revised version:
'O Lord grant that we may not be like cornflakes - lightweight, brittle and cold; but like porridge - warm, comforting and full of goodness.'

On a small island off the West Coast of Scotland they tell the story of the old minister who used to pray: 'A blessing on our beautiful island, and on the neighbouring islands of Great Britain and Ireland.'

Lord, on whom all love depends,
Let us make and keep good friends.
Bless me also with the patience
To endure my wife's relations.

A Mr. Kernan tells how after a severe snowstorm had closed all the schools in their area, the teacher asked an eight-year-old boy if he had used his extra time constructively. 'Yes Miss', he replied, 'I prayed for more snow.'

Bishop Desmond Tutu of South Africa, the 1984 Nobel Peace Prize-winner, was celebrating Holy Communion at the Grace Episcopal Church in New Orleans, during a visit to the United States. He ended by pronouncing the benediction in Xhosa. Sensing that some of the congregation were puzzled, he smiled and added, 'I assure you, He understood.'

A Cyclist's Prayer

Lord, Thou who hast never ridden a bicycle, help those who have to. Only Thou knowest the dangers we are subjected to and the difficulties we go through. Help us on the upward slopes. There is no need to push us downwards. Sustain us when we go through a deep hole full of water that seemed a shallow hole. Deliver us from dogs that like to run after us to bite the wheels. And above all, **help us to buy a car.** Amen

Dr. Luccock tells of a mother who showed her little girl the moon shining early one afternoon. 'We usually see it at night' she said, 'but there it is in the daytime.' The little girl was perplexed. In her prayer that night, she said, 'Oh Lord, you made a big mistake today.'

Abraham Lincoln told of a little girl who received beautiful alphabet blocks. She liked them so much that she played with them that night in her bedroom until she was very sleepy. Then she remembered she had not said her prayers. So she knelt by her bedside and prayed. 'Oh Lord, I'm too sleepy to pray, but there are the letters. Spell it out for yourself.'

Shortest Scottish grace: 'Heavenly Pa, Ta!'

Doubtful Compliments

How numerous are the doubtful compliments which have been paid to ministers.

'I don't care what other people say, I like your sermons.'

'If I had known you were going to be good today, I would have brought a friend.'

'You always find something to fill up the time.'

'It's not that you preach longer than others. It just seems longer.'

'That was a great sermon today. For once I felt you did not mean me.'

The Very Rev. Dr. Andrew Herron tells how during his ministry in Houston, Scotland, he once engaged the services of a professor as a guest preacher for a special anniversary service. Later Dr. Herron asked one of his members, an experienced sermon-taster, what he had thought of the professor. 'Oh verra guid, verra guid,' said Willie, 'verra learned, aye maist awfu learned. But ye ken what I'm gonna tell ye? Ye're every bit as guid yersel in yer ain ignorant kind o' way.'

When his popular television lectures were being screened, Professor William Barclay, that most prolific of Christian writers, took his wife for a holiday to Troon. At breakfast one morning, an American lady came over and enquired whether he was the Professor Barclay who was giving those wonderful television lectures. When Dr. Barclay admitted he was, she asked if he had a church of his own. He told her that he had not, intending to explain that he taught students studying for the ministry, but before he could do so, she put her hand on his shoulder and said, 'Don't worry. I'm sure you'll get one soon.'

22

Walking home from church with a hard working farm labourer who was a regular worshipper, the minister congratulated the man on being present each Sunday in the pew. 'Oh, I enjoy the Sunday service.' he replied. Just as the minister was experiencing what some call an 'ego-inflation', the labourer continued, 'Sunday for me really is a day of rest. I works hard all week, and then I comes to church on Sundays, and when you start the sermon, I puts my feet up on the heating pipes under the pews, and thinks o' nothing.'

A minister one Sunday preached a sermon that was greatly admired by a fellow-minister. To his surprise a few days later the second minister found the same sermon in a book of sermons published in America ten years previously. When he next met his minister friend, he said to him, 'What rascals these Americans are. I have just discovered they have taken the sermon you preached last Sunday and published it - ten years ago!'

One Sunday after an illness which left me temporarily deaf, I happened to say to one of my office-bearers, 'That was a strange experience. I could not hear myself preach.' 'My' he said, 'You were lucky.'

In the pulpit one Sunday there was a visiting minister who had the body of a Colossus, the brain of a child and a voice whose bleat was so faint it was the despair of even the front pew. Professor Cairncross tells how on the Monday the parish minister asked one of his more thoughtful members, how he had enjoyed Mr. Watson. The member hesitated. The recollection was obviously painful and difficult. Then with considerable deliberation, he said, 'Yon's what I would ca' a strong weak man.'

A visiting bishop spoke at America's Yale University on the four letters Y, A, L and E. He held forth for ten minutes on Y for Youth, for seven minutes on A for Ambition, for five minutes on L for Loyalty - by which time he had lost his audience - and then for a few minutes on E for Energy. The comment of one young man who was present was, 'I'm just glad I go to Yale and not the Massachusetts Institute of Technology.'

A parish minister in West Lothian had an exceptionally loud voice. One Sunday he preached in a neighbouring parish. One man said to another as they walked away from church, 'What did you think of that oratory?' 'Man,' was the reply, 'that was not oratory. That was roaratory.'

The late Dr. Alexander Findlay, who was a distinguished New Testament scholar, went on one occasion to preach at a church, the main door of which was reached by climbing a flight of steps. That morning at the bottom of the steps there was an elderly lady. With characteristic courtesy, Dr. Findlay offered his arm. Together they slowly ascended the steps. When they finally reached the door the old lady turned to her escort and asked, 'Do you happen to know who is preaching this morning?' 'Dr. Alexander Findlay' was the reply. 'Oh' said the old lady, 'would you mind helping me down the steps again.'

An Alfred Williams tells of an old lady who sat in the front of their church. Each Sunday she would hold the minister's hand at the door after the service and say, 'Mr. Scott, that was a beautiful sermon.' If the sermon was lacking in quality she would identify some part of the service: 'Mr. Scott, that was a beautiful prayer.' She always found something nice to say. But one Sunday everything seemed to go wrong. He had had an exceptionally busy week and had been up all Saturday night trying to reconcile a divided family. That day she took his hand, look up and said, 'Mr. Scott, that was a beautiful text.'

Dr. Andrew Herron tells of once visiting an old fellow who said, 'They have not gotten you on the wireless yet.' With fitting modesty Andrew explained, 'No, they have not got down to my level yet.' At once the man sprung to his defence, 'I wouldna let you say that. Na, na. I wouldna let you say that. They had an awfu' puir man on last Sunday.'

A widow, whose daughter was about to sit her finals in medicine, was explaining to the local minister how difficult it was, how they did not want you to pass nowadays, how anything was a good excuse for failing you, and so on. 'Oh', said her minister anxious to be sympathetic, 'I know how the standards are constantly going up. Why even in divinity since my day the whole thing is much more difficult.' To which the hostess kindly replied, 'Maybe it's just as well you got through when you did.'

Bishop Renfrew tells how he gave a portrait of himself which he really could not stand having in his own house, to the nearby Catholic school. A few days after it was put up in the front hall in a gold frame, a little lad was found gazing at it. The Chaplain who was passing said, 'Do you know who that is?' 'No father, I haven't a clue', said the boy, 'but it is probably a dead Pope.'

A Norfolk vicar told an elderly parishioner that he would soon be retiring and would be very sorry to leave. 'But', he assured her, 'you will probably get a better man.' 'Not necessarily', she replied comfortingly, 'that is what the last one said before he went.'

To another minister who was moving to a new parish, an elderly lady suggested that his successor would not be as good as he had been. 'Nonsense', he replied flattered. 'No really', insisted the old lady. 'I have lived here under five different ministers and each one has been worse than the last.'

A young Manchester priest tells how he chose matrimony as the topic for his first sermon. Greeting parishioners in the porch afterwards, one elderly lady said to him 'Well Father I only wish I knew as little about it as you do.'

A former Elgin minister tells how he called one day to visit a gentleman who was ill. Before taking him in to see her husband, the wife told Mr. Cowan that her husband was very ill and wandering in his mind. When she finally took him into the sick room, she leant over her sick husband and said, 'Here is Mr.

Cowan to see you.' 'Oh aye, Mr. Cowan', he mumbled, 'a fine man and a grand preacher.' 'Now', said the woman turning to Mr. Cowan, 'didn't I tell you he was wandering.'

It was towards the end of the 19th century that Scottish Presbyterian ministers began to wear academic hoods in the pulpit. The Rev. Dr. Walter Ross Taylor wore a red D.D. hood when he acted as moderator of the Free Church Assembly, and afterwards in his own church in Glasgow. One Sunday a woman in the congregation had a friend with her. Uncertain if it was Dr. Taylor who was going to be conducting worship that Sunday, they were watching the vestry door. 'Is it him?' the visitor asked in a whisper. 'Aye, aye, it's himself with his jeely bag on his back.'

A Highland farmer who had attended for the first time the General Assembly, that annual gathering of Church of Scotland ministers in Edinburgh, was asked on his return home for his

impressions. After giving the matter due thought, he replied, 'Ministers are rather like dung. They are all right when spread thinly over the land, but get them in a heap and they are a bit nauseous!'

William Johnston, a former Moderator, tells how an elderly lady once said to him, 'I'm glad to meet you. I have heard you often on the wireless. It's funny from the voice you imagine what the speaker is like. But now that I see you, you're not at all what I imagined. On the wireless you have such a *young* voice.'

The Rev. Stewart Lamont tells how as a divinity student he once preached on Easter Sunday in Inverarity Kirk, Angus. 'I gave it big licks. The trumpet did sound a certain note! Afterwards the Session Clerk entered the vestry. There was a pause in which he felt a verdict needed to be given. 'Well that was certainly different today.'

Mr. Lamont also tells how his college friend, the Rev. Finlay Macdonald, also did the Angus Church circuit. Like many divinity students he often preached the same sermon in different churches. At that time he had a beard which he later shaved off after becoming engaged. One day at Belmont Eventide Home a lady greeted him warmly after the service. 'Mr. Macdonald, I did not recognise you at first without your beard - but then I remembered the sermon.'

Bishop John Mone, one of the Auxiliary Bishops in Glasgow visited a school one day. When one little boy told his mother later that night about the Bishop's visit, she enquired which of the three Glasgow bishops it had been. The wee lad thought for a moment. 'Gosh it was that new one, but I can't remember his name. I think it was something like nark.' (Nark is Scots slang for Moan!)

Holy Wit

Boyd Scott tells of a minister in the Church of Scotland General Assembly who stood up and proposed a motion. 'Mr. Moderator', he continued, 'I had arranged for a seconder, but he has since taken ill.' Looking around the Assembly Hall, the Moderator said, 'Well, is anybody else willing to take the risk?'

Lewis Browne, the author of books about the religions of the world, was a rabbi before he decided to become a writer. One day at a literary dinner, a rather sceptical rabbi asked Browne about his theological beginnings. 'You were a rabbi eh?' When Lewis Browne replied in the affirmative, the man then asked, 'Were you unfrocked?' Browne had a quick answer. 'No', he said, 'just unsuited.'

It used to be compulsory for all Anglican students at Trinity College Dublin to attend chapel on Sundays. Hoping to exempt himself from this rule, one young rebel claimed on his application form that he was a 'Sun Worshipper'. Early on his first Sunday morning at college, he was awakened by persistent knocking. Bleary-eyed he opened the door to the college porter, who said respectfully, 'The Dean's compliments Sir. The sun will be up in five minutes and he expects you in the Front Square to see it rise.'

The young people in the church decided to raise money by having a car wash. On the morning the car wash was to be held, it was pouring with rain. The vicar saved the day by putting up the sign: 'God's cooperative Car Wash. We wash - He rinses.' The venture was a great success.

A church warden complained to Bishop Stubbs of Oxford that the curate in his parish wore a hood somewhat like that of an Oxford M.A., which he was not. 'The man has a lie upon his back, my Lord', said the angry church warden. 'Don't say a lie Mr. Smith', replied the Bishop. 'Say rather a false-hood!'

A minister stopped at an historic American hotel and requested rates for a single room. When he was informed that a room on the first floor was 75 dollars, on the second floor 65 dollars and on the third 55, he said,'Thank you' and made to leave. 'Don't you like our hotel?' the receptionist asked. 'Oh it is beautiful', said the minister. 'It's just not tall enough!'

Jean Henderson was the first woman ordained by the Beaver-Butler Presbytery in America. When her first baby was due, a resolution was sent from the Presbytery giving her permission 'to labour within the bounds of the Presbytery.'

Bishop Magee a former bishop of Peterborough, went on one occasion to Worthing to recuperate after a serious illness. On leaving the hotel he asked for his bill. Though it seemed exorbitant, he paid it without complaint and in addition gave the waiter a tip. As he was leaving, the manager said, 'I hope your Lordship has found the rest and change of which you were in need?' 'Unfortunately I have not', replied the bishop. 'The waiter has got the change. You have got the rest, and I have got nothing.'

Father McCann, a priest from Bangor in Northern Ireland, had for some time been plagued by a man who kept coming to see him or phoning him whenever he had a drink too many. On one occasion Father McCann recognised the familiar voice when he lifted the phone. Disguising his own voice, he said, 'Just a minute and I will see if Father McCann is in.' Putting down the phone he then went outside for a few moments, took a few deep breaths of fresh air, and then returned to the phone. 'I am sorry', he said. 'He was outside a few moments ago, but he is no longer there.'

Many ministers try to avoid meeting in public places with those under the influence of alcohol, for often such a person will either pour out his soul, or ask the most difficult theological questions when in no fit state to receive any kind of meaningful answer. Dr. Lauchlan Maclean Watt, a former minister of Glasgow

Cathedral once travelled back from Edinburgh to Glasgow on a crowded evening train. Just before the train left, a drunk man entered the compartment and sat down directly opposite Dr. Watt. Hoping that he hadn't noticed his clerical collar, Dr. Watt raised his newspaper to hide behind it. But the man had noticed, and was in a talkative mood. Shortly after the train started, the drunk man said in a very loud voice, 'Padre, do you know something? I don't believe in heaven.' Dr. Watt paid no attention. A few seconds later, in a louder voice, he said, 'Padre, don't you hear me? I don't believe in heaven.' Again Dr. Watt said nothing. Finally the drunk man pulled down the paper and said, 'Padre, do you not hear me? I don't believe in heaven.' Slowly raising his eyes, Dr. Watt said, 'Well, go to Hell, but go quietly.'

A tourist who had returned from Rome told how a priest-guide had shown them round the catacombs. At one point in the tour a youngster had asked the priest why some of the passage-ways were roped off. When he was told that there were miles and miles of tunnels and one could easily get lost, the boy's eyes widened at the thought. 'For ever and ever?' the boy asked in an earnest voice. 'Amen', intoned the priest-guide.

A minister who was asked if it was a sin for an average family to own two cars and a boat, replied, 'It would depend where they were parked on a Sunday morning.'

Another minister was overheard to say, 'I never had any difficulty recruiting Primary Sunday School teachers, not since the day the primary pupils started going out of church before the sermon and offering!'

Dr. Potter, a former bishop in New York, was asked by a young lady why angels were always portrayed in pictures or stained glass as either women or young men with beards. The bishop's reply was a marvel of diplomacy. 'My dear girl', he said, 'everyone knows that women naturally inherit the Kingdom of heaven, but men only get in by a very close shave.'

Another story about Dr. Watt tells how one day as he was walking up the High Street in Glasgow he heard a woman's screams coming from a near-by tenement. Climbing the stairs he found a husband beating his wife. Pulling them apart, he finally restrained the man by forcibly sitting on him. When the husband recognised who he was, he said, 'Dr. Watt if you just get off me, I will join your church.' At that moment a policeman, who had been summoned by a neighbour, came in the door. Seeing the minister of the Cathedral sitting on the man, he inquired of Dr. Watt whether he was having trouble. 'No', said Dr. Watt, 'I am just conducting a communicant's class.'

The Rev. Johnstone Mackay, whose father was a controversial figure in the Kirk, once took part in a debate in Paisley Presbytery. When he had finished speaking a fellow minister rose to his feet and said that if Mr. Mackay Jr. went on saying things like that, he would make enemies. On hearing this, another Presbyter said with a twinkle in his eye, 'That is the last thing Mr. Mackay needs. He inherited enough.' (Told by the Rev. Johnstone Mackay on B.B.C. Radio.)

For many years Angus Mackenzie was the minister of Stoer and Assynt, two tiny churches in North West Scotland. Mr. Mackenzie was not only a fine preacher, but an equally fine fisherman. On one occasion when the Bishop of Bath and Wells was on holiday in Sutherland, he contacted Mr. Mackenzie and asked if he would like to spend some time with him on the river. In return he could perhaps give him a few lessons on fly-fishing. The two men were soon good friends and on first name terms. When at the end of the holiday the bishop returned to his diocese, he wrote Angus the most delightful letter of thanks. He then proceeded to sign it as he did his business letters, 'Bath and Wells'. In his reply Angus expressed his thanks and then mischievously signed it, 'Stoer and Assynt'.

Dr. Andrew Herron once assured the General Assembly, 'There are two sides to every question. My side and the wrong side.' This remark reminded some of the long argument between two friends about their denominational differences. The argument was concluded when one remarked, 'Well I suppose you will just go on worshipping God in your own way, and I will go on worshipping Him in His.'

A much more humble minister said one day to a friend, 'Some of us have the pleasure of seeing our congregations nod approbation while they sleep.'

Dr. Tom Simpson after being installed as Moderator of the Presbyterian Church in Ireland, said, 'The office of Moderator is for one year only. I suppose it was based on Aristotle's maxim that 'He whose term is short cannot do much harm.' He also recalled how St. Patrick in his early days tended the sheep on Slemish Mountain a short distance from his birthplace in Ballymena. 'Like myself, St. Patrick left the area while still a very young man. All wise men come from Ballymena, and the wiser they are, the quicker they come!'

A Lincolnshire vicar who had read in a report of the ecclesiastical commissioners that about six-sevenths of the clergy stipends are paid from the church's endowments, said to a friend, 'I feel like telling my people that when they have had two sermons from me on a Sunday they have had their share, and if I spend the other six days pottering around the churchyard, that is fine, because that is where most of the people are who pay me.'

At a special service held in Falkirk to commemorate the fourth centenary of the Scottish Reformation, the preacher saw fit to attack the Roman Church in fiery language. When it was moved at the next Presbytery meeting that two prize essays written by young people on a Reformation theme, might be mimeographed and sent to various interested parties, to the dismay of the Presbytery, the preacher suggested that copies of his sermon might be enclosed with them. The strained silence which followed was finally broken by Mr. Leslie, then the minister of the Old Kirk in Falkirk, rising to his feet and saying, 'That is not possible. You are not allowed to send inflammable material by post!'

In the days before Church of Scotland ministers had to retire at 70, one elderly Glasgow minister struggled on, even though he was far too frail and old for the job. Being however a most likeable old man, no one wanted to hurt his feelings by suggesting that he might retire. But finally one Sunday several of the office-bearers met with him at the close of the service. As gently and graciously as possible, one of them said, 'We are not hearing you very well these days. Have you never thought of retiring?' They were speechless when he replied, 'And do you really think you would hear me any better if I retired?'

'If God had planned to allow today's permissiveness, He would have given us, not Ten Commandments, but Ten Suggestions.'

'Some look at the Ten Commandments as an exam paper: eight only to be attempted.'

Each year the opening ceremony of the General Assembly is attended not only by churchmen but also by civic dignitaries and many press reporters. On one occasion the retiring Moderator Robin Barbour, said of his successor, Bill Johnstone, who was much smaller of stature, that when he thought of Dr. Johnstone the text which immediately came to mind was one from the Zaccheus story. 'He sought to see Jesus who he was; and could not for the *press*, because he was of little stature.'

A clergyman who was given a flowery introduction began his reply by saying, 'May the Lord forgive this man for his excesses, and me for enjoying them so much.'

Billy Graham once said that 'A Christian should so live that he would not be afraid to sell the family parrot to the town gossip.'

Professor Murdo Ewen Macdonald once told how he and the new minister of St. Giles in Edinburgh, the Rev. Gilleasbuig Macmillan, attended an official dinner shortly after Mr. Macmillan had moved from Portree, a delightful Highland village on the Isle of Skye, to the historic High Kirk of Edinburgh. Sitting next to Mr. Macmillan was a lady from the top-drawer of Edinburgh society. At one stage in the evening, she said, 'Accustomed as you have been to preaching in Portree you must find it very different preaching to the members of St. Giles.' Mr. Macmillan's reply was not quite what she expected, 'Yes. I have had to simplify my sermons considerably.'

Saint Thomas More's sense of humour sustained him right to the steps of the scaffold. He accepted help climbing up, but joked that 'as for coming down I will fend for myself.' He then asked the headsman to let the axe spare his beard since it, at least, had not offended King Henry.

In his *Scottish Reminiscences*, Dean Ramsay recalls how it was common for ministers in rural parishes to bow at the close of the service to the heritors who often occupied the front seat of the gallery. A Dr. Wightman of Kirkmahoe was once criticised for neglecting this usual act of courtesy. On the Sunday concerned the laird's pew contained a bevy of ladies, but no gentlemen. The minister who was a bachelor omitted the usual salaam in their direction. A few days later, meeting Miss Miller, who was widely famed for her good looks, and who afterwards became Countess of Mar, he was asked why he had not bowed to her and her friends the previous Sunday. 'I beg your pardon Miss Miller, but you surely know that angel worship is not allowed in the Church of Scotland.' Raising his hat he walked on.

A missionary bishop of the Church of North India, addressing one of many meetings in England, said with feeling, 'In heaven there will be no partings; I hope there will be no more meetings.'

While addressing the crowd at Speaker's Corner in London's Hyde Park, the distinguished Methodist minister Lord Soper was interrupted by a heckler who kept shouting: 'What about flying saucers?' Finally Lord Soper turned to him and, much to the delight of his audience, silenced him with:'I cannot deal with your domestic difficulties now.'

A minister was tossing a coin with one of his office-bearers to see who would pay for the coffee. When asked if that did not constitute gambling, the minister replied, 'It is merely a scientific method of determining who is going to commit an act of charity.'

Professor H.H. Mackintosh used to warn his students against overloading a sermon. He likened an overloaded sermon to a pipe which has been tightly packed with tobacco. 'It will not draw.' Then he would add. 'When a pipe is packed too tightly, it is usually filled with someone else's tobacco!'

When Bishop Feaver of Peterborough received a letter addressed to 'Bishop Fever', he added a P.S. to his reply. 'I am not now or ever have been a disease.'

Gas and Gaiters

The warm relations that exist today between church leaders did not exist in 19th century Glasgow. Walking one day through the city with a friend, the Very Rev. Dr. Norman Macleod noticed the Roman Catholic Archbishop approaching with his valet, both dressed in black from head to toe. Although Dr. Macleod smiled as they passed, there was not a glimmer of a smile in return. When his friend asked, who was accompanying the Archbishop, Dr. Macleod informed him with a twinkle in his eye, 'That is the valet of the shadow of death.'

Archbishop William Temple loved to make a 'joyful noise to the Lord'. During his time as Bishop of London, he was one night passing a mission church. Going in he joined the congregation. The hymn being sung had a swinging tune. The bishop joined in lustily. But finally the man standing next to him could stand his raucous voice no longer. Unaware of who William Temple was, he said, 'Look. Would you dry up minister? You're spoiling the show.'

Pope John XX111 came of farming stock. His father had struggled to make ends meet on his little farm. During his time as Cardinal, he once recalled his father's hard life. Then with a flash of humour added, 'There are three ways of ruining yourself - wine, women and farming. My father chose the most boring.'

Around the time of his 80th birthday in 1961, Pope John wrote, 'I notice in my body the beginning of some trouble.' Told by doctors that he had a 'gastropathic condition', he smiled and said, 'That is because I am Pope. Otherwise you would call it a stomach ache.'

Dr. James Moffatt, renowned for his translation of the Bible, was a former pupil of Glasgow Academy. Like many who were educated at the Academy, he was a keen rugby enthusiast. On one occasion he was asked to open a Church Sale of Work.

Unfortunately on the day of the Sale, the Academicals were due to play their great rivals, Heriots, at Anniesland. Torn between desire and duty, he nevertheless opened the Sale. At church the following day one pious lady was describing the occasion to her neighbour. 'We were fortunate to have Dr. Moffatt with us. He is such a busy man he had to rush away after opening the Sale to attend an open-air meeting at Anniesland.'

Professor Arthur Gossip and Dr. Henry Sloane Coffin, the president of Union Seminary in New York, were life long friends. Their friendship began when Arthur Gossip was welcoming the foreign students to New College, Edinburgh. That day he casually mentioned that some people enter the ministry with a fearful handicap. 'My handicap is my name. I doubt if any one could have a worse name for a minister than Gossip.' (This was in the days before Cardinal Sin of the Philippines came to prominence!) From the back of the hall an American student said, 'I will take you up on that. My name is Coffin.'

Years later Dr. Coffin was sitting in the President's office in Union Seminary, when the phone rang. The voice at the other end said, 'Is that Union Cemetery?' 'Yes', replied the President, 'and it is Coffin speaking.'

Billy Graham's country upbringing and humour is reflected at times in his sermons.
'A woman once told me all her little boy needed was a pat on the back. I told her if it was low enough and hard enough it could do him some good.'
'Perhaps teenagers have too much leisure time. That was never a question in my youth. I got up at 3.a.m. to milk the cows and when I got out of school I had to milk the same cows. Some how they had filled up again!'

Dr. Graham also recalls the first time he ever went North to hold meetings. He was with a friend from Alabama. Neither of them had ever been North before. When they stopped one day at a filling station, the attendant came round and filled up the tank. 'Then he asked my friend from Alabama, 'How's your oil?' And my friend replied, 'We're all right, how's you all?'

Dr. Carlyle Marney, one of the prophetic figures in the American Church, was gardening one Monday morning at his home in Charlotte. It being a damp wet morning he was wearing old waterproofs and an old hat. Suddenly there was a screech of brakes as a chauffeur driven cadillac drew up beside where he was working. A very aristocratic lady got out from the back seat, came over to him, and thinking he was the gardener, inquired in a very condescending manner how much he charged. 'Ma'am', he replied, 'I don't charge anything. The lady of the house simply lets me sleep with her.'

When Dr. George Macleod, the founder of the Iona Community, was asked how the biography he was hoping to write was progressing, he replied, 'Not very well, but at least I have a good title - *By George!*'

At the service of thanksgiving which was held to mark the 90th birthday of Dr. Macleod, Uist Macdonald told how in the thirties, the Communists of Red Clydeside knew George well but thought his remedies for Govan's considerable social problems were merely palliative. 'Come the revolution' said one of them, who secretly respected Dr. Macleod, 'all ministers will be strung up on the nearest lamp-post. But in your case we are prepared to make a concession. We will be willing to come to your funeral.'

In the T.V. programme, *Your Adversary the Devil*, the Very Rev. Hugh Douglas had arranged for some photographic enlargements of devilish characters to be used in the introduction. One of these was Da Vinci's 'Prince of Hell'. During the rehearsal an inexperienced caption operator got his captions in the wrong order. The result was that the moment the 'Prince of Hell' was seen glowering from the screen, the superimposed caption mistakenly read, 'Dr. Hugh Douglas'.

This was a great source of innocent merriment in the studio. Some time later when Dr. Douglas was visiting a lady who had viewed the programme, he told her of the mistake in rehearsal. Her comment was, 'To tell you the truth, I thought the picture was rather like you.'

The Rev. Dr. Henry Ward Beecher once preached a controversial sermon against slavery. Two days later he received a letter which contained one single word, 'FOOL'. Commenting on the letter he said, 'I have known many instances of a man writing a letter and forgetting to sign his name, but this is the first case I have known of a man signing his name and forgetting to write the letter.'

Professor George Adam Smith, the distinguished Biblical scholar, told how as a young minister, he was once invited to conduct a communion service in a little country church in Aberdeenshire. The Presbytery clerk who made the arrangements had informed him that the church was effectively run by two men, the local laird and a retired colonel. He also told George that at the end of the service, one of them would give him a sovereign and the other would take him home for lunch. All happened as he had been told. The laird gave him the sovereign and the colonel invited him for lunch. Only later did he learn that these two pious looking gentlemen had a private wager. Whoever was last finished serving his side of the church with the bread and wine, got off with giving the sovereign. The other, the loser, had to take the visiting minister home for lunch.

Dr. Halford Luccock who for many years was a distinguished figure in the American church, tells how when he was eight years old he became an atheist. Along with other eight-year-old converts to atheism, they decided to prove their atheism by burning a Bible. Having collected wood and paper Halford placed on the fire the black bound book from his father's study. Not only did it not burn as easily as they thought it would, but in the middle of the 'convert ceremony', Halford's father returned home early. When he asked for an explanation, they told him

39

that having become atheists they had decided to burn the Bible. To their further disappointment, he pointed out that the book they had on the fire was not a Bible but a dictionary!

The Rt. Rev. Bill Westwood, shortly after being appointed Bishop of Peterborough, wrote from his rambling 12th century Bishop's Palace, the setting for television's *Barchester Chronicles*, to thank his former area for their generous parting gift. He said it would be used to buy useful things for his new home - chairs, carpets, tables . . . and a compass!

Archbishop Runcie, when Bishop of St. Alban's, was being driven one day to officiate at a church dedication. On the way he noticed in a butcher's window some magnificent hams. Pressed for time, the chauffeur was reluctant to stop, but promised he would on the way back. On the return journey as they parked outside the shop he noticed that the butcher was beginning to close for the day. Rushing into the shop, followed by Dr. Runcie

at a more sedate pace, the chauffeur inquired if there was a ham for the bishop. Signalling to Dr. Runcie to come round behind the counter, the butcher whispered, 'If you change our vicar, I will give you a whole pig!'

Shortly after Archbishop Runcie's celebrated meeting with Pope John Paul at Canterbury, he was invited to address the General Assembly of the Presbyterian Church in strife-torn Northern Ireland. Outside the Assembly hall a number of protesters carried banners which read, 'Archbishop Runcie is a Romaniser.' Noticing that the Archbishop was upset by these placards, one of the welcoming party sought to cheer him up. 'It might have been worse. The placards might have said, "Archbishop Runcie is a Womaniser".'

A former Bishop of Southwell tells of a fellow bishop watching a football match. When a goal was scored, he was heard to exclaim, 'That shot was richly blessed.' The Bishop of Southwell's comment was that he thought that was an ecclesiastical idiom for the more familiar, 'That was a damned good shot.'

In 1982 Cardinal Basil Hume delivered the opening address each day at a week long retreat for American bishops. The event took place in Minnesota. At the conclusion of the conference the bishops gave Cardinal Hume an unusual gift. It was a T-shirt inscribed with the words, 'It's a boy.' That day Diana, Princess of Wales had given birth to a son.

Stewart Lamont tells how he was once invited to be a guest preacher in the Dundee Congregational Church at Meadowside, where many of the non-Presbyterian denominations have their buildings. 'I arrived expecting the Rev. George Gahagan to greet me. Finally I decided to go down into the vestry to change as the time was approaching 11 a.m. and the Kirk was filling up. I went to the loo. On coming out, I saw a board lying in the cloakroom with the name of the then chairman of the Methodist Synod in Scotland. The penny dropped. I was in the wrong kirk!

I tore up the stairs, fully robed, through the church and out into Meadowside past an astonished Methodist minister greeting his incoming congregation. I arrived at the Congregational Church which was fifty yards along the road with two minutes to spare.'

'I'm going to the Plaza' is a common Glasgow saying indicating you are going to the famous Glasgow dance hall. Bishop Charles Renfrew tells how he had to go one night to the Plaza in full Bishop's regalia to accept a cheque from some Roman Catholic Benevolent Society. 'It was a Friday night. The official car which was supposed to collect me, failed to arrive and I was forced to summon a taxi. Imagine the look on the taxi-man's face on a cold November night, when I climbed into the taxi in my vestments and said, 'Take me to the Plaza.' Looking at me rather strangely, he said, 'You must be joking.' 'Well' said I, 'just kid on it's a fancy dress ball and take me all the same.'

Bishop Black, who for some time was the R.C. Bishop of Paisley, was a very humorous character. When the Queen came to Scotland one very hot June day, the Press got a good photograph of him talking to the Queen. The Queen was roaring with laughter. For a long time he refused to tell what he had said to make the Queen laugh so heartily, but later confessed that when the Queen had said, 'Bishop, you must feel very warm in these robes on a day like this', he had smiled and replied, 'But your Majesty, you don't know what I have *not* got on underneath.'

On another occasion Bishop Black arrived in solemn procession in his Cathedral to find the marble gates of the altar firmly closed. From the back of the procession he said, 'When I say three, jump.'

When the late Dean of York was asked why he had called his stumpy-tailed fox terrier, Mark, he exclaimed, 'The New Testament contains the life-stories of our Lord by Matthew, Mark, Luke and John. Mark's is the shortest tale!'

Religious Clangers

In the 1960's the St. Andrew Press produced a study booklet for the Women's Guild entitled *The World's Children*. That year at their annual rally in the Usher Hall, Mrs. Grieve, the National President, said she would like publicly to thank Tim Honeyman the director of St. Andrew Press, for his cooperation with the Women's Guild in the production of the world's children! The following morning Mr. Honeyman found a little note on his desk from one of his less reverent friends, 'I always wondered what went on in this room.'

The Very Rev. George Duncan, the year in which he was Moderator of the Church of Scotland, was invited to say a few words at the centenary celebrations of a temperance society. In his distinctive sheepish voice he said, 'Ladies and Gentlemen, this is a great day in your history, a hundred years old today. Why you remind me of that other great Scotsman, Johnnie Walker, still going strong.'

Two American tourists who were visiting York were horrified to hear about the recent fire at the Minster. 'Gee, how dreadful. Pity it wasn't on this week.'

A minister who had returned one Sunday to a former charge, went to the door at the close of the service to shake hands with the worshippers. To a lady he recalled well, he said, 'Jean, how is your husband?' When she replied, 'Oh John is in heaven', he was so stunned that he blurted out, 'I am very sorry to hear that.' Then realising what a silly thing he had said, he tried to correct himself, but simply made matters worse by saying, 'No, I mean I am surprised.'

From the church magazine of All Saints' Church, Kings Langley: 'Vicar is on holiday until the 27th. Clergy from the Parish of Berkhamstead will be celebrating on the Sundays when he is away.'

During a period when industrial unrest threatened the smooth running of funerals in the cemetery normally used for Christian burials in Bombay, the lady in charge, a Miss Dyer (!) sent out the following memo. 'During the period of the strike, the cemetery will be operated by a skeleton staff.'

From another church magazine:'The Rev. John McNeill left Liverpool on Saturday for Toronto where his future work in the Presbyterian Church in that city is *to lie*.'

An audible titter ran round the church when the minister said, 'I want to say a few words before I begin.'

During an Assembly debate on whether the minister's home should be a public or private place, the Very Rev. John R. Gray rose to his feet and said fervently, 'My manse has always been a public house.'

A minister who was involved in a minor accident with a cyclist, stopped his car and rushed back to apologise. Anxious to make amends, he gave the cyclist one of his calling cards, saying that if ever he could be of assistance the man had only to contact him. When the cyclist arrived home he found the card read, 'The Rev. J. Smith is sorry he missed you today.'

The Ely Diocesan magazine *Contact* quoted with delight a local newspaper report:'The sudden gust of wind took all who were at the ceremony completely by surprise. Hats were blown off and copies of the Vicar's speech and other rubbish were scattered over the site.'

An English church publication received the following reply to a 'Help Wanted' advertisement: 'I am applying for the advertised position for an organist and choirmaster, either lady or gentleman. I have been both for many years . . .'

A minister one day relinquished his seat on a crowded bus to an inebriated soldier who was being criticised by many of the passengers for his failure to keep his feet in the passageway of the bus. 'Thank you minister', said the inebriated warrior. 'You are the only person on this bus who understands what it is like to be drunk.'

From the pulpit of a Methodist Chapel in West Yorkshire the following advice was given: 'And so my friends, whenever I am up against it, I just take my courage in both hands and the grace of God in the other.'

An old lady said to the Rev. James Dow. 'I loved your autobiography. I hope you will write another.'

Anne Evans tells of a man who called one day at the manse in Elgin and handed in a bag of sticks. Not knowing who he was, Anne inquired if anything special had prompted the gift. 'Well it is like this. Your husband recently did me a great favour. He buried my wife.'

A Scottish minister who had once in his own church preached a very effective sermon on the text, 'Naaman was a commander of the Syrian army, *but* he was a leper', decided to preach the same sermon during an American exchange. What he did not realise was that the word butt in America refers to a persons posterior! The three points of his sermon were:
'Everyone of us has a but.'
'It is easy to see other people's buts.'
'It is difficult to see your own but.'
The congregation had difficulty hiding their amusement.

A minister began the service by saying, 'We are very pleased to welcome those visitors who have come to worship us.'

Another minister who was encouraging his congregation to face religious issues head on said, 'We must be *sharp and to the point*. We must be *blunt*.'

At a church meeting the deteriorating condition of the rectory windows was discussed. Finally a motion was passed. 'We move that a committee be appointed to look into the rectory windows.' *Anglican Digest*.

A Canadian choir director was teaching the new anthem. 'Don't forget', he said. 'You wait until the tenors reach the "Gates of Hell" and then you all come in.'

When the Christian education department of a large American denomination decided to use the American standard version of the Bible in their church magazines instead of the King James version, the version authorised by King James 1 in the 17th century, one man wrote, 'I don't want any new translation. I want the Bible the way the apostle James wrote it.'

Notice by Vicar in parish magazine. 'We are thinking of forming a branch of the Mothers' Union in the parish, so any ladies wishing to become Mothers should meet me in the vestry after the service.'

Mrs. Anne Evans tells of inviting Stanley Baxter with whom she had once worked closely on the radio, to open their annual Sale of Work. Stanley Baxter, Jimmy Logan and Andy Stewart were at that time Scotland's three best known entertainers. On the day of the Sale, Stanley Baxter told Anne how on the last occasion he had done this, the minister who was introducing him had gone on at great lengths about his career in acting. After what seemed like an eternity, the minister had said, 'Now I will call on Stanley *Logan* to open the Sale.'

One New Year Sunday a Helmsdale minister rebuked his church officer, not only for arriving late for the evening service, but also for being the worse for drink, and for falling asleep during the sermon. The man excused himself by saying that he had been up the Strath that afternoon, and then added, 'You know what it is like at New Year.' 'I know perfectly well' replied the minister. 'I was up the Strath myself this afternoon visiting, and I am not in the state that you are in.' 'No', agreed the beadle, 'but you are not as popular as I am.'

A minister announced, 'It may be of interest to those who have children and don't know it, that there is a nursery downstairs each Sunday.'

For many years Helen Kerr was a missionary nursing sister in the hospital at Mlanje, in Malawi. Helen tells of receiving, along with other missionaries, a questionairre to complete from the Church Offices concerning, 'The Movements of Missionaries.' She and the other members of the hospital staff were strongly tempted to reply, 'Regular.'

The church officer at Whalley Church in Lancashire was showing some American visitors round the building. He was asked for what purpose a certain path had been used. 'It is a bit uncertain' he said, 'but they do say the monks and nuns used to walk along it when they were courting.'

Of Such is the Kingdom!

Each Sunday the minister would call the children to the front of the church. There he would show them something or tell them a story. Once he had a telephone to illustrate the idea of prayer. 'You talk to people on the telephone and don't see them on the other end of the line - right?' The children nodded, 'Yes.' 'Well, talking to God is like talking on the telephone. He is on the other end, but you cannot see him. He is listening though.' Just then a little boy piped up and asked, 'What's God's number?'

Children have an uncanny way of reducing the inexplicable to their own terms. A child explaining how God creates people: 'He draws us first, then cuts us out.'

The child describing what a halo is: 'They have this circle of light over their heads and they always try to walk careful so that they stay right underneath it. It lights up.'

The child who heard the story of the Prodigal Son for the first time: 'In the midst of the celebrations for the Prodigal' said the teacher, 'there was one for whom the feast brought no happiness, only bitterness. Can you tell me who this was?' 'The fatted calf', suggested one little lad.

A youngster when asked why there are no longer burnt offerings to God, suggested, 'Air pollution.'

A minister showed a painting to a child. 'It is not really Jesus', he explained, 'just an artist's idea of him.' 'Well it certainly looks like Jesus', said the child.

The family was on the way home from church. 'What did you learn at Sunday school today, Freddy?' asked his mother. 'Some silly song about Jesus wanting me to be a sunbeam.' 'What is silly about that?' asked his mother. 'Because I want to be a bus driver.'

Mr. Alston, a teacher of religious education, tells of teaching the story of the prodigal son to a class of thirteen year old boys. Towards the end of the lesson he got the boys to write the story in their own words. One boy wrote, 'In the far country the prodigal spent most of his money on wine and women, and he wasted the rest.'

A little boy told by his mother that he might go on a picnic she had previously forbidden, sighed, 'It's too late, Mummy. I've already prayed for rain.'

A minister in his children's talk on Easter Sunday asked the children how big they thought the stone was, that was placed in front of Jesus' tomb. All kinds of sizes were suggested. To the boy who suggested that it was the size of the pulpit, the minister said, 'Yes that would be about the size.' To his next question, 'Who do you think could move a stone that size?' he got the answer, 'The Council.'

One little lad thought 'false doctrine' was what happened when the doctor that was called in 'made a bloomer'.

When a child was asked what one must do before obtaining forgiveness for sin, he replied, 'Sin'.

When asked what are some of the things you could do without in Lent, one little boy replied, 'Soap'.

In the School nativity play in which the children had been encouraged to express the story in their own way, the inn-keeper having told Mary and Joseph that there was no room at the inn, immediately added, 'But come away in for a drink anyway.'

The Sunday school lesson was on 'friendship'. Mr. E.J. Ball of Northland Church, Darlington, asked his class of ten-year-olds to give him another name for 'friend'. When Andrew suggested 'pal' and Iain said 'chum', Matthew chipped in with: 'They're not friend words, they're dog foods.'

A minister who was telling the story of the lost sheep, asked the children, 'Why do you think the shepherd left the ninety-nine sheep, possibly to the wolves and the lions and went out to look for the one that was lost?' 'Because it was probably the ram', said one wee lad.

A little boy came home from Sunday School and informed his mother that his new teacher was Jesus' Granny. When asked how he got that idea, he replied, 'Well, she never stops talking about Jesus.'

Leonard Small tells a story of a little boy who set off for Sunday School and Church one morning with two coins in his pocket - one for the Church collection and the other for the Sunday School. That night as his mother was folding up his clothes one of the coins fell out of his trouser pocket. Convinced that her boy was on the road to a life of crime, his mother asked him to explain how the coin was still in his pocket. 'Well, Mum', he said, 'I met Grandpa outside the church and he paid me in!'

A teacher from Saltash tells how his teaching career started in a draughty classroom opening onto the school hall. While writing on the blackboard one day he heard a child come in and sit down, leaving the door wide open. 'And who was born in a barn?' he enquired loudly. Quick as a flash came the reply, 'Jesus, Sir.'

A minister who had called on the congregation to bow their heads in prayer, was interrupted by a young voice asking excitedly, 'What are we looking for?'

Just before Christmas my young son was practising for the lesson he was to read at the Church carol service. With a perplexed look on his face and a typical child's disregard for the sacredness of the Holy Book, he said, 'Mum, there is a mistake here. It says Mary was great with child. Surely it means 'great with children'?

A Robin Reames tells how he once attended a service where the visiting preacher gave a sermon on the symbol of the dove. It was directed mainly at children. At one point he tried to coax from the young people what the dove stood for.

'It is gentle', ventured one child.

'It is pure', suggested another.

'Anything else? asked the preacher.

'It eats our cabbages', said another boy!

A Glasgow lady tells how though her grand-daughter was an enthusiastic member of the Church Brownie pack, she was also very much a child of these labour saving times. One evening she came home after a pack meeting and cried in despair: 'I've got to wash a pair of socks to qualify for a badge, and I don't know how to work the washing machine.'

When the Presbyterian Church in Ireland elected Ronald Craig as Moderator, his grandson was overheard telling friends, 'My grandfather has been made the radiator of the church.'

A small boy on his way to church for the first time was being briefed by his elder sister.'They won't allow you to talk', she warned him. 'Who won't?' asked the boy. 'The Hushers.'

One little lad thought the Pharisees were a breed of horses, because it said in the Bible, 'Woe to the Pharisees.'

A teacher was telling her children one Sunday that God was a Spirit. Next Sunday by way of revision, she asked them who God was. None of them could remember, but one bright specimen finally held up his hand and said, 'Whisky'.

Edward Thompson who ministers in Scotland but hails from Northern Ireland, tells of asking the children one Sunday in Church what their favourite Bible story was. One unexpected reply was, 'Jesus healing the ten lepricorns.' (lepers).

One little boy got his prayer muddled and in consequence said, 'Let my friends be all forgiven. Bless the sins I love so well.'

Shortly after the birth of Prince Harry, I asked the younger children in Dornoch Cathedral if they could tell me who the baby's Mummy and Daddy were. The children had no difficulty in answering. They also were able to tell me who the baby's Granny was, but when I asked them who the baby's grandfather was, not a hand went up. By way of giving them a clue, I said, 'It is the Duke of something.' Immediately one wee lad shouted out, 'The Grand old Duke of York.' Collapse of congregation.

The Sunday School teacher at West Plains United Church, Burlington, Ontario, announced to her class that the Sunday School was having a Christmas party. There would be a special guest - someone with a fat tummy? Did any of the children know who it would be? One little girl put her hand up promptly, 'It must be the minister.'

A Sunday School teacher had been telling her class about the armour of God - the breastplate of righteousness, the shield of faith, the helmet of salvation, and so on. 'There is something else we must carry', she added, referring to the sword of the Spirit. When no one answered, she said, 'Well it is very sharp and it cuts.' On hearing this one little girl's face brightened and she said, 'Is it the axe of the Apostles?'

A father tells how his football crazy son expresses everything in terms of the game. When the church service one Sunday had been going on for ninety minutes, he pointed out how it was 'full time'. Then came prayers for the sick. 'Now' he whispered, 'we are in injury time.'

A little boy arrived home from Sunday School in tears. 'What's the matter', his mother asked. 'Teacher asked all those who wanted to go to heaven to put up their hands.' 'And did you put up your hand? said his mother. 'No' he sobbed, 'You told me to come straight home.'

Youngsters heard in Woolworth's at the cards counter. 'These aren't Christmas cards. These are holy ones.'

The Sunday school teacher told the story of the Good Samaritan with all the dramatic details of the robbers, the blood, the dirt, the flies. Then she asked her kindergarten class what they would have done if they had come upon the poor merchant lying in the ditch. Finally one little boy replied 'I fink I woulda frone up Miss.'

With the youngsters gathered round his feet, the minister was reaching the climax of his story: ' . . . and as they entered the forest, they saw something big and black and terrifying climbing up a tree in front of them. Have you any idea what it might have been?' A small boy replied 'It was Jesus. It's always Jesus.'

A Sunday School teacher asked her class how they thought Noah might have spent his time in the ark. When there was no response, she asked, 'Do you suppose he did a lot of fishing?' 'What', piped up a six-year-old, 'with only two worms?'

Taptisms

A five-year-old came home and told her parents about the 'taptism' she had seen in church. 'Do you know what it meant?' asked her father. 'Sure', she said, 'the baby got tapped on the head with water.'

The Rev. John Cameron tells of taking his three-year-old son to the Church prior to the morning service to help prepare for a baptism. The wee lad poured out the water and carefully laid a small towel beside the font. During the service, just prior to the actual baptism, the wee lad was heard to shout out, 'Daddy we have forgotten the soap.'

When one of Andy Stewart's children was christened in St. John's Renfield Church, Glasgow, the huge carving knife which the church officer used to prize out the silver bowl for cleaning, was left at the side of the font. Andy must have wondered whether for Melanie it was going to be New Testament baptism or Old Testament sacrifice.

Studdert Kennedy (better known as Woodbine Willie) tells of a baby who had been given the Christian names Alfred Homer. When making the customary entry in the baptismal register, the minister paused thoughtfully when he came to the second name. The couple being simple working class folk, the name Homer surprised him. Turning to the proud father the minister said, 'Is Homer your favourite poet Mr. Brown?' 'Poet Sir?' said the man with a surprised look. 'Poet, lord no. I keep pigeons.'

A Mrs. Christison tells of taking her three-year-old grand-daughter, who was staying with her and her husband, to a christening. It interested her greatly. A few weeks later they were invited to a wedding. Again they sat her at the end of the pew so that she could see everything. As the bride came down the aisle, a small voice said in a very audible whisper, 'Where's the baby?'

One wonders if it was an unfortunate baptismal experience which prompted Bishop Douglas Feaver to say that people's love for babies amazed him. 'All they do is leak at both ends.'

Stanley Mair, the former minister of Netherlee Church, Glasgow, very much longed for a little girl. The Sunday after his fifth son was born, he informed the congregation that he and his wife were strongly tempted to christen their new baby boy, 'Nay' .... Nay Mair!

A family from Dornoch on holiday in Edinburgh visited Waverley Market where their seven-year-old daughter was fascinated by the coins lying in the ornamental pool. The following day, being Sunday, they attended Charlotte Baptist Chapel and were seated in the front pew with a full view of the baptismal font. When the collection was announced, the little girl turned to her Daddy and whispered, 'Do we throw our pennies into the water?'

I Plight Thee My Trough

Lutherans in the United States were spurred on to consider updating the marriage service by a recollection from Lavern Grosc. He heard a young farmer tell his bride, 'I plight thee my trough.' (troth) 'I knew', he said, 'that she would always be well fed.'

At a wedding in an Anglican church the young bridegroom who was from a relatively poor home was heard to repeat the well-known words 'With all my worldly goods I thee endow.' On hearing this, his father turned to his mother and whispered, 'There goes his bicycle.'

A cartoon in the *Wall Street Journal* featured a wedding ceremony in which the minister was saying: 'Do you Tom and Valleri, promise, I mean really promise, I mean honest-to-goodness, solemnly, cross-your-heart-and-hope-to-die promise, not to go running off like spoiled brats to the divorce courts after your first row?'

A bridegroom who was a keen football supporter was upset that his wedding coincided with his team playing a vital cup tie. During the reception he kept inquiring if the waiter knew the score. When finally informed that his team had won 3-1, he turned to the minister and said, 'Oh it has not been such a bad day after all.'

While writing a book *Marriage Questions Today*, I decided to deliver a series of Sunday morning addresses on marriage and its related questions. One of my members who brought her elderly maiden aunt to church each Sunday, phoned her on the Saturday night to inquire whether she would be going to church the following day. When greeted with a rather stony, 'Why not?', her niece reminded her that the sermon was to be about marriage. To this her aunt replied, 'Well I'll just go and see how fortunate I have been.'

The Rev. John Sutherland, a former minister of the Gallowgate in Glasgow, told of returning home late one night. It was shortly after the end of the Second World War, and the lights were not yet fully back on the streets. As he walked along a drunk man attached himself to him. When they came to a part of the street where there was more light, the drunk man turned and looked more closely at Mr. Sutherland. Then with great venom in his voice said, 'You are the B . . . that married me.'

Another Glasgow minister tells of being wakened early one Saturday. At the door stood an anxious young man and a distraught middle-aged lady. 'Mr. Grieve', she said, 'you know you were due to marry my daughter this afternoon. Well something terrible has happened. She had a baby in hospital last night. After discussion, Mr. Grieve agreed to marry the couple in the maternity hospital that morning.This having been done he then went to the church to inform the many guests that the wedding had taken place, but that the reception would go ahead

57

as planned. Mr. Grieve says he will never forget the reception, for no sooner was the meal over than one of the guests rose and proposed a toast to 'absent friends.'

James Currie tells of a private wedding he conducted. Unknown to him the best man had just been released from Borstal the previous week. When Mr. Currie presented him with the Bible to place the ring on, the lad placed his hand on it instead, and raising his other hand said, 'I promise to tell the truth, the whole truth and nothing but the truth, so help me God.'

A minister who during the marriage service suddenly forgot the bridegroom's name, looked him straight in the face and in a very ministerial voice asked, 'In what name have you come here today.' Taken aback by this unexpected question, the lad finally said, 'I have come here in the name of the Lord Jesus Christ.' The minister was no further forward.

To a Highlander of advanced years who had decided to get married, his minister said, 'Well Donald, I trust you have got a hand-maid of the Lord.' 'Indeed minister', said Donald. 'I dinna ken whether she's hand-made or machine made, but she's gey weel put thegither.'

The wedding report in the local paper said, 'The bride wore a long white dress which fell to the floor.'

Marry and you get a new leash (lease) on life.

The game of love has altered little from cave-man days. They just changed the trumps from clubs to diamonds.

A bride's mother from London tells how the bride and groom posed for the usual photographs outside the church after their Easter wedding. When the photographer brought the proofs, there were roars of laughter. In many of the pictures the 'wayside pulpit' on the side of the church was clearly shown. Its message was, 'Father forgive them; for they know not what they do.'

As a happily married man, I have long taken the view that in domestic arguments or discussions the male should have the final word. In my case this has always been 'Yes dear' or 'Of course dear' or 'I could not agree more dear.'

Asked during a television interview what was the best advice he had ever been given, a minister said that it was that he should marry the girl who was now his wife. 'Who advised you to marry her?' was the next question. The reply was, 'She did.'

The young girl was thrilled to be invited to her cousin's wedding, including the party afterwards. When asked if she had been to a wedding before, she replied, 'I've been to the church part before, but never to the conception.'

A Mrs. Weiss remembers how she came out of the church having just married a navy lieutenant. She turned to him for those first precious words with which to start their marriage. 'You're out of step', he said.

Humorous Marriage Epitaphs

'Here lies Obidiah Wilkinson and his wife Ruth.' Underneath were the words: 'Their warfare is ended.'

An American left instructions for the following epitaph to be inscribed on his tombstone:

Here I lie beside my two wives,
Lilley and Tilley.
I loved them both
But let me tilt towards Tilley.

On an old British tombstone there is inscribed:

The children of Israel wanted bread
And the Lord he sent them manna.
Old clerk Wallace wanted a wife
And the devil sent him Anna.

Dead Funny!

Samuel Upham who taught at Drew Seminary in the 19th century, was much loved for his wisdom and unconquerable wit. As he lay dying, sober friends and relatives gathered about his bed. Some questioned whether he was still living. 'Feel his feet' one advised. 'No one ever died with warm feet.' Dr. Upham opened one eye. 'John Hus did.' he said. Those were his last words.

On his way to a funeral in a hired car, the minister leaned forward and tapped the driver on the shoulder to ask him a question. When the driver visibly jumped, the minister apologised for startling him. 'That's all right sir', the driver replied. 'It's just that I usually drive the hearse.'

At a Highland funeral one of the mourners who was slightly the worse for wear, fell into the grave on top of the coffin. When they got him out, they discovered he had broken his leg. The local paper in reporting the incident said, 'Unfortunately this accident cast an atmosphere of gloom over the proceedings.'

A former headmistress tells of meeting with the local cemetery supervisor to choose a lair. It was her intention not to be a financial burden to her relatives when she should die. Showing her round the cemetery, he said, 'I would not choose this corner. It gets very wet in the winter time!'

A lady from Lochinver was showing distant relatives from Canada round the local cemetery. 'That is where your uncle Willie is buried', she said, 'and there is where your Aunt Maggie is buried, and that is where, if I'm spared, I'll be buried.'

'When do you think we might be able to introduce these changes?' asked a minister to one of his younger office-bearers. Aware of the resistance to change of some of the older office-bearers, the young man replied, 'Well, I guess there will have to be some prominent funerals first.'

When the 5th Duke of Sutherland died his body was flown home from the Bahamas in a huge ornate casket. The coffin, the like of which many Sutherland folk had never seen before, was scarcely an hour in Golspie before one local wit had christened it the 'juke (duke) box'.

'Mr. Jones believed that the secret of his eternal youth lay in the fact that he had an early morning jog followed by a long walk every day. The funeral takes place next Tuesday.' (*The Kentish Times*)

An Anne Jewel of Swansea tells how her boss who had had a minor scrape with his car, had asked her to telephone the garage to find out whether the repairs had been completed. She asked the switchboard operator to contact them. When the call was duly answered, she said, 'Could I speak to someone in the body-shop, please?' There was a 'deathly hush'. 'Madam', a stony voice replied, 'this is Swansea Crematorium.'

A Shropshire newspaper contained the following note of 'grave' concern. 'The old churchyard has been sadly neglected largely because there have been no burials there for more that fifty years. An appeal is to be launched to encourage volunteer bodies to remedy the situation.'

Why didn't Noah kill these two mosquitoes when he had the chance?

A Mrs. Browner from Warwickshire, tells how while an elderly parish priest was tending his garden near the local convent, a pedestrian stopped to enquire about his much loved roses. 'They are not bad', said the priest, 'but they suffer from a disease peculiar to this area know as the "Black Death".' Anxious to increase his gardening knowledge, the passer-by asked what on earth that was. 'Nuns with scissors', replied the priest.

A man from Leicester tells how he was asked to arrange the transport of a coffin from Dublin to the west coast of Ireland. The only way to take it was by train, so he telephoned the Irish Rail office to enquire the fare. 'Certainly sir', the girl replied, 'Was it single or return?'

The mailing label for a magazine was returned from the Post Office marked: 'Deceased. Address unknown.'

A hotel manager employed a wee Glasgow chap to wash and polish his car every Saturday for 50p. The wee man died suddenly, and the manager went along to the tenement flat in the Gorbals to pay his respects. The mourners were seated, not saying a word, when a face appeared round the door, topped by a flat bunnet. 'I'm the corpse's brother' the man said, 'and I'd like you all to come through tae the kitchen tae drink his health.' Without a word or sign of surprise, the entire company rose and followed him.

Home Truths

A lady I once visited woke from an afternoon nap to see me standing by her bedside. Several thoughts obviously flashed through her mind, for she said, 'Oh Mr. Simpson, I nearly did not recognise you. You see, I haven't my teeth in!'

An old lady who had learned that her soldier son was in hospital and that one of his nurses was in fact the daughter of a neighbour, remarked to her minister, 'It's a wee world. Just to think o' oor Willie's broken leg being in the hands of a kenned face.'

A minister near Aberdeen told of a woman who had been ill. When he called he genuinely thought she was looking much better, but surprisingly she was not pleased to hear this. 'No, No', she said, 'I'm far from well. Only a Higher Hand knows what is going on in my inside.'

On several occasions when the husband has answered my knock at the door, he has said, 'I suppose it is my wife you have come to see.' The implication that I am the local Casanova worries me!

A Mrs. Booth from Preston tells how her husband, a Methodist minister, once went to visit a church member who had gone into hospital for an operation. He arrived in the ward to discover the man still shaking off the anaesthetic, and promised to come back the next day. 'Do you remember me coming yesterday?' he asked on his return visit. 'Yes' came the reply, 'I vaguely recall seeing you and thinking, 'I can't be in Heaven, because there is Mr. Booth.'

An elder tells of calling on an old lady shortly after the induction of their new minister, the Rev. Bill Macmillan. Mr. Macmillan's wife was an *anaesthetist* in a city hospital. Discussing their new minister, the old lady expressed her regret however, that such a fine minister should have a wife who was an *atheist*.

Dr. Norman Macleod was one of the best known ministers in the Scottish Church in the 19th century. He was a great favourite with most people in Scotland as well as Queen Victoria, acting as her private chaplain for many years. Ian Maclaren tells how on one occasion the minister of the neighbouring parish was summoned to see a man who was dangerously ill. Having visited the man in the bedroom, the minister then had a word with his wife. 'I fear your husband may have typhus fever.' 'Aye, Aye', the wife replied with mournful pride. 'It's no ordinary trouble.' Then he inquired if they had been long associated with his church, for he had not recognised the man's face. 'No' she replied, 'We go to Norman's church.' 'That's fine,' he said. 'You could not go to a better. But why did you send for me?' 'Lord bless you sir! Do you think we would risk Norman with typhus fever?'

During a visit which the Queen Mother made to Baxter House, one of the Church's Eventide Homes, one of the residents, a contemporary of the Queen Mother, took her by the arms and said, 'I know some of your relatives'. The Queen Mother who seems never to be at a loss for words, said, 'Oh that is interesting. Which of my relatives do you know?' The church officials who were accompanying the Queen Mother were more than a little embarrassed when the lady said, 'Oh I did like the Duke of Windsor.'

A Highland minister, engaged in collecting money for a new church, got a few likely names from Dr. Whyte of St. George's. Taking the first name on the list, he called at the house of an eminent doctor and was shown into a handsome drawing room. When the doctor said he could not afford to give a subscription, the minister pointed to the grandeur of the room in which they sat. At this the doctor lost his temper. 'Do you know who I am?' he said hotly. 'Yes' replied the minister stoutly; 'just a hell-deserving sinner like myself.' Whereupon the doctor rang the bell and ordered him to be shown out. Overwhelmed by such a defeat at the very outset, the minister returned at once to Dr. Whyte and told him what had happened. 'What! You told him he was a hell-deserving sinner like yourself - you told him that?' exclaimed Dr. Whyte with a glint in his eye. 'Well' he said, 'For that I will give you five pounds myself and I'll give you another five if you'll go and say the same to Dr. . . . ,' naming another eminent physician.

The Very Rev. Dr. James Matheson tells how he was asked by a member of the congregation, a devout lady, to see her husband in hospital. He had stubbornly insisted that he was an atheist, and would have nothing to do with the church. With him being terminally ill, she hoped that he might be able to help him face the fact. 'I went with some reluctance.' said Dr. Matheson. 'In spite of my best efforts I failed entirely to get through to him. Finally I said 'I must go now. Would you like me to pray with you?' 'No' he said, 'but you could do something for me. I cannot reach the radio switch up there. Would you turn it on. I have some money on the 2.30 and it's just coming up!'

Tom Allan used to tell of once being left in the sitting room with a four-year-old while his mother went to make a cup of tea. The wee lad kept looking at him and then finally said, 'You're not good looking.' When the mother returned, the minister thought he would make a joke of it. 'Your wee lad was telling me that I am not good looking.' 'Oh' said the mother, 'You always get the truth from children, don't you?'

A newly ordained woman minister who had been conducting worship in a Scottish country church, was invited with the local minister to Sunday lunch at a nearby farm. The farmer's wife had cooked a chicken which they all enjoyed. After lunch the farmer showed his guests round the farm. As they passed the cock, it began to crow like mad. 'Seems very proud of himself', commented the woman minister. With a twinkle in his eye the farmer replied, 'No wonder, he has now got a daughter *in* the clergy.'

Bishop Mone once went to an orchestral concert rather late one winter's evening. Having been that afternoon at a special

consecration service, he had his precious crosier with him in his car. Rather than leave it there, and possibly have it stolen, he took it into the hall in its leather bag. The concert had already started when he arrived. The doorman took one look at the muffled figure and said, 'Hey Sir, I don't know what instrument you are playing, but you are a devil of a late.' What a wonderful picture - an orchestra of Bishops playing crosiers.

Rosehall must be one of the most remote villages in Britain. Robert Alston who was a minister in this peaceful Highland village for several years, tells how he was once offered home-made whisky while out visiting. When Mr. Alston said, 'You know John, this is not altogether legal.' His host replied, 'Oh Mr. Alston, the law has lost its sting before it reaches Rosehall.'

Voting for God

A child who was describing the difference between Jews, Protestants and Catholics said, 'They are all just different ways of voting for God.'

A group of ministers attending a Conference had a free afternoon. Despite the wet weather they decided to go for a walk. They came to a ricketty derelict footbridge crossing a burn which was in full spate. Suddenly they heard a shout and saw an old man running down the hill towards them. The senior minister shouted back, 'It is all right, my man. We are not trespassing. We are Presbyterian ministers from the conference.' Back came the reply. 'I am not caring whether you are Presbyterians or not. I'm simply telling you that if you try to cross that bridge, you'll all be Baptists.'

In the 19th century the Established Church in Scotland owned a considerable amount of land. Often round the manses there were glebes which the minister either farmed himself or rented out. On one occasion a country farmer who attended the Established Church went to the Free Church minister and asked him to pray for rain. This gentleman asked him why he did not go to his own minister. The farmer replied, 'Na, na, ye'll nae catch him praying for rain for my neeps, when his ain hay's nae in yet.'

The distinguished Presbyterian minister Dr. Carnegie Simpson did a great deal at the beginning of the century to build bridges between the Anglican Church and the Presbyterian Church in England. On one occasion he invited a Canon who was staying with him to accompany him to an open air meeting which was being held in the Presbyterian Church of which he was minister. The Canon declined, saying that he did not know how the Bishop would feel about it. Then partly to soften the impact of having declined, he said, 'But may God go with you.' On hearing this, Dr. Simpson smiled and said very graciously, 'If it's all right for God to come with me, would it not be all right for you?'

A Protestant minister, who had dropped in to visit a Roman Catholic priest in his rectory, remarked, 'Father you have such comfortable quarters here, so much better than my parsonage, that I envy you.' 'Yes', replied the priest with a smile, 'You ministers have your better halves and we priests have our better quarters.'

A Scottish farmer brought up in the Presbyterian church, went on one occasion to a service in St. Paul's. Never having seen an English prayer book, he spent his time before the service examining it. He had not long been doing this when suddenly he replaced the book, picked up his hat and left. He later explained to a friend that as he had turned over the leaves of the prayer book, there was nothing but 'Collect' and bits of prayer, and then 'Collect' again. 'If I had stopped for all these collections,' he said, 'I wouldn't have had a penny left.'

An Earl Nielson of Canada tells how he and his wife were invited to a bar mitzvah. Arriving slightly late at the synagogue, they sat down beside a man with kind eyes, who sensed they were unfamiliar with the service. The rabbi was reading and the man opened a prayer book for them, with English on one page and Hebrew on the other. He also indicated where the rabbi was in the text. 'These are the laws of Moses', he whispered. Mr. Nielson nodded, but perhaps did not look too sure, for he repeated, 'Moses. You know - Charlton Heston?'

Some years ago a local Roman Catholic priest took part in a carol service with ministers of different denominations in the town. When he got into his car after the service, it refused to start. Passers-by were treated to the sight of a Catholic priest, an Anglican clergyman and a Methodist minister pushing an old car along the street. 'This', one of them commented, 'is called an ecumenical movement.'

Dr. James Matheson, a former Moderator, tells how he once had a call from an undertaker. An old lady in the parish had died. Would he conduct the funeral? 'I went along at once and found a family who claimed to be Church of Scotland. They seemed to be a loving united family and it was easy to talk with them and pray with them. After the funeral I went as usual to call at the house. As I went in two nuns fluttered out. In some confusion the family admitted that they were Catholics, but their mother who had 'turned Catholic' for her marriage, made them promise that she would be 'buried a Protestant'. They were afraid that if I knew about it, I wouldn't conduct the funeral. I told them that would have made no difference to me, but that they should have told me. I later told the story to a priest who was a good friend. "That's tit for tat." he said. "Early this morning I was called to the Western General Hospital to give the Last Sacrament to a man who was dying. When I got to the ward a nurse showed me the bed with the screens all round. Man it was difficult to get him to make his confession. Hard work it was. But I managed at last and gave him the Sacrament. When I was leaving the Sister said, 'Here you are Father. The man who wants the Last Sacrament is through here.' "I'd given the last rites to a Protestant. Never mind James, they'll sort out the books up there".'

A discussion is reported to have taken place between a priest, a protestant minister and a rabbi concerning when life began. The priest was in no doubt that it began at conception. The minister felt it really began at birth. 'Look' said the rabbi, 'You have both got it wrong. Life begins when the dog dies and the kids leave home.'

Bishop Charles Renfrew once introduced himself by saying, 'Renfrew and Paisley are two Scottish towns near Glasgow. Often in the past I have been introduced as the Bishop of Paisley instead of Bishop Renfrew. Though the two towns may be geographically close, I assure you that Charles Renfrew is poles apart from what Ian Paisley says and does.'

A saying in America: 'The Baptists rescue people from the gutter - The Methodists clothe them - The Presbyterians educate them - The Episcopalians teach them the social graces and the Baptists once again rescue them from the gutter!'

'It often happens that I wake at night and begin to think about a serious problem and decide I must tell the Pope about it. Then I wake up completely, and remember that I am the Pope.' (Pope John XX111).

A guest at a party got jostled and half his glass of beer landed on a R.C. priest. His other black suit being at the cleaners he was concerned that he would have to conduct mass the following day smelling of beer. A helpful lady offered him some perfume that she had in her purse, to mask the smell of the beer. After a moment's consideration, the priest said, 'No thanks. The beer I'm allowed. The perfume might raise all kinds of questions.'

Hymnastics

Someone suggested the Church Choir Practice might be called 'Hymnastics'.

A member who was tone deaf once told me that the hymn that brought him greatest comfort when he thought of the life to come, was, *I love to hear the story*. The reason, he said, is that glorious line, 'That *even I* may go to sing among his angels.'

While carol singing in the local hospital, one of my members asked me why each Christmas I insulted the congregation! Assuring the person that it was certainly not deliberate, I asked her to explain. 'Well' she said, 'Each Christmas you intimate that the children will sing the first verse of *Away in a Manger* and that then the congregation will join them for the second verse, 'The cattle are lowing.'

J.B. Philipps in his book *Price of Success* tells how 'Many hymns tickled my all too easily roused sense of humour. I mention one because it haunted me for years. In one of the verses, we sang to the Almighty, 'Lord give me Samuel's ear.' I did not want Samuel's ear and would not know what to do with it if I had it. But the hymn writer not only asks for an ear, but specifies which one he wants - 'the open one O Lord'. That was and is too much for me.'

W.I. Croome, a distinguished expert on church architecture, tells how in his village they had no street lights when he was a boy. The light from the shop windows partially compensated, shining as they did out on to the pavement - except on Thursdays when the shops shut for their half-day. Then it was a dark journey home from school. During the winter, as he journeyed home on Thursdays, he used to sing the hymn with the line, 'Grant us every *closing* day, light at eventide.'

On one occasion the veteran cricketer W.G. Grace played against Marlborough College School. He was bowled for a 'duck' in the first innings and a small score in the second. At evensong in the chapel that evening there was considerable hilarity when the boys noticed in the hymn they were singing the line, 'The scanty triumphs grace hath won.'

In 1937 East Fife football club, who play at Methil, defeated Kilmarnock in the Scottish Cup final. The celebrations at Methil went on into the small hours of Sunday morning. Later that morning one of the local ministers, a keen supporter of East Fife announced that they would begin the service by singing the second paraphrase, 'O God of Methil' (Bethel) and that they would sing it to the tune 'Kilmarnock'!

Paul Robinson of Manchester tells how he and his fiancee were discussing what hymns to have at their wedding. Paul's fiancee, a small girl, just 5ft. tall, said, 'My favourite hymn is *All Things*

Bright and Beautiful. Her father on hearing this looked at all 6ft. 3ins. of Paul and said, 'You must be joking - the next line is 'All creatures great and small.'!

The members of the General Assembly of the Church of Scotland were highly amused when it was pointed out that in the printed list of hymns they had been given, the hymns for inclusion in the new hymn book, the first two hymns of the Funeral section had unfortunately been included as the last two hymns of the Marriage section. One of them began, 'Go happy soul, thy days are ended.'

Choirmaster to Choir Boy: 'No, no, Carruthers, the hymn writer was Wesley, not Presley.'

At the conclusion of a Mother's Day sermon about honouring mothers all the year round, one minister announced the closing hymn, *This is my Father's World.*

The choirmaster of a church in Nairn tells how he had long complained about the poor lighting over the piano he plays for the choir practice. But then one evening, when he entered the hall, he found a beautiful new angle-poise lamp perched on top of the piano. On the music rack was a hymn book open at the hymn, *Sometimes a light surprises the Christian while he sings.'*

A choirmaster pointed out that if you listen to any congregation singing the hymn with the line 'that our weak hearts no more may stray.' It sounds remarkably like 'that our wee cats no more may stray.'

A little lad who was almost tone deaf surprised his mother by informing her one day that he had almost been picked to sing a solo at the school service. The mystery was solved when he added, 'The boy next to me was picked.'

World Without End

A Dr. Parr was once invited by the Lord Mayor of London to preach at a special civic service. He went on for a very long time. After the service the Lord Mayor rebuked the minister in a most telling way. 'There were four things in your discourse which I did not like to hear.' 'What were these?' asked the astonished doctor. 'The quarters of the church clock which struck four times before you finished.'

A long-winded country minister once informed a parishioner that he was intending to preach the following Sunday on the milk of human kindness. 'Well', said the farmer, 'I hope you will give it to us in condensed form.'

'Ministers who think by the inch and talk by the mile, deserve to be kicked by the foot.'

At an especially long church service one Sunday, a service in which the minister exhausted time and encroached upon eternity, a small voice was heard asking at the back of the church, 'Mummy, is it still Sunday?'

Dr. Black of St. George's, on going to preach in a country kirk, was asked by the beadle, 'Hae ye your sermon written?' When the reverend gentleman replied that he had, the beadle exclaimed, 'I'm real glad, because when you folk come wi' a paper, we ken you'll stop when it stops; but when ye hae nae paper, the Almichty Himsel' disnae ken when ye're likely tae feenish.'

A stand-in clergyman went way back into the hills to conduct a service at which one man proved to be the entire congregation. The preacher asked the man if he thought they should go on with the service. The man pondered, then replied, 'Well Reverend, if I put some hay in the wagon and go down to the pasture to feed the cows and only one cow shows up, I feed her.' So the clergyman went through most of the service including a full-length sermon. Afterwards the man said, 'Reverend, if I put some hay in the wagon and go down to the pasture to feed the cows and only one cow shows up, I don't give her the whole damn load.'

Ministers entering the pulpit should write at the top of their manuscripts, the words of the Negro Spiritual, 'I ain't got long to stay here.'

'Can our Society Survive?' was the subject of the sermon. After listening to the gloomy preacher drone on for forty-five minutes, one worshipper nudged his neighbour and whispered, *'No'* is the word he is groping for.'

The printer's error was very much to the point. By substituting unintentionally an 'n' for an 'r', it described a certain longwinded minister as 'The Neverend Mr. Jones.'

The minister announced that if the congregation reached the fund raising goal, he would allow a clock to be installed in the pulpit. If the offerings exceeded the goal, he even promised to look at it!

During a series of sermons which Dr. Ralph Sockman once gave on the life and teaching of Jesus, the following notice appeared one Sunday on his church noticeboard:

11.00am 'The Greatest Preacher in the World'
Dr. Ralph Sockman

He took a long time to live that down.

In 1963 when the Los Angeles Dodgers were due to play the New York Yankees in the World Baseball Series, a New York preacher chose as his topic, 'The Dodgers can't win'.

The memorable title of a Christmas sermon preached by Dr. Ralph Nesbitt was 'Wise men always worship'.

Another memorable sermon notice was **God's last name isn't damnit. Come and find out more about this god.**

The minister's small daughter was watching her father prepare his Sunday sermon. Finally she asked, 'Daddy, does God tell you what to say?' 'Of course', he answered smiling, 'why do you ask?' 'I was just wondering why you score out so much?'

The following advice concerning preaching was once given to a young minister. 'Be sure you begin with something good and be sure you end with something good and let the two be as close together as possible.'

Have Another One

A Christmas Eve service was being considerably disturbed by a man who had been celebrating Christmas Eve in a very different fashion. Finally the beadle walked over to the man and whispered something to him. The drunk man got up at once and quietly left the church with the beadle. When the minister later inquired how he had got him out of the church so easily, he replied, 'It was quite simple. I merely asked him to come out and have another one on me.'

Church beadles often had a 'guid conceit o' themselves'. When one of them was asked if he could recommend a good beadle for another church, he replied, 'Weel sir, had it been a minister body that was wanted, there's plenty o' them; but a beadle sir, a beadle's no sae easy got.'

An office-bearer of the church was once heard to say, 'I dislike modern translations of the New Testament on the grounds that St. Paul is best left incomprehensible.'

The stained glass windows in Hyndland Church, Glasgow, make artificial light a necessity for worship. One Sunday on arriving to conduct worship there, I discovered the church was being rewired, and that there was no electric light. A smile came over the faces of some of the worshippers when I announced my text. 'If your very light turns dark, how great is the darkness.'

On a poster outside a church: If it didn't rain, there would be no hay to make when the sun shines.

Looking rather scruffy after one of his frequent walking tours, C.S. Lewis, one of the most prolific writers of the 20th century, boarded a train for the journey home. An old lady in one compartment asked him snootily, 'Have you a first-class ticket?' 'Yes madam', replied Lewis, 'but I'm afraid I need it for myself.'

A tramp who called at the manse asked for a drink. When the minister's wife brought him a glass of water, he said, 'I'm not dirty. I'm thirsty.'

A former choir member was asked by his minister why he had given up singing in the choir. 'I was absent one Sunday' he said, 'and somebody asked if the organ had been mended.'

A minister was watching two boys pushing a heavy cart up a country hill. 'If you were to push it zig-zag, you would find it much easier.' 'Sir', said one of the boys, 'it would go up much easier if you were to come and give us a shove.'

A minister once asked an elderly man who had moved into the district if he participated in any sports. To the astonishment of the minister, he replied, 'No, my parents won't let me.' 'Your parents?' questioned the minister. 'Yes' he replied, 'Mother Nature and Father Time.'

A worshipper entering church one very wet morning noticed that the verger was ringing the bells more vigorously than usual. He asked the reason. 'If they are not coming to church', replied the verger with a twinkle in his eye, 'They're not sleeping either.'

Silence is golden . . . A 'sponsored silence' by the Sunday School of Kirk o' Field Parish Church, Edinburgh, raised £191.00 while another in Dunfermline Abbey brought £183.00. Asked how they organised it so successfully, those taking part said, 'We're keeping quiet about it.'

The old lady was deaf. This meant that the question she asked her minister was asked sufficiently loudly for everyone in the room to hear. 'Was entering the ministry your own idea, or were you just poorly advised?'

A Roman Catholic bishop tells how it is not uncommon for a bishop who is staying the night in a hotel, and who has in his suitcase a rochet for use in a religious ceremony the next day, to find his pyjamas and the rochet (a close-fitting surplice which resembles a lace nightdress) laid out on different sides of the double bed!

A paid attendant at one of the great English Cathedrals was asked by an American tourist, 'Excuse me, is this place open on Sundays?

On the day of Princess Anne's wedding, we were invited to a neighbour's house to watch the Royal wedding in colour. Sitting beside me was my six-year-old son Graeme, whose great love at that time was playing simple card games with his brother and sister. That day he sat and watched intently as the *kings* and *queens* from all over Europe arrived at Westminster Abbey. Suddenly the Archbishop of Canterbury appeared in his magnificent gold robes and mitre. Graeme, being the son of a Presbyterian minister, had never seen anyone dressed like that before. Pointing to Archbishop Ramsay, he said, 'Daddy, is that the *Joker*?'